J.R TOLKIEN

A LIFE INSPIRED

Introduction

John Ronald Reuel Tolkien was Professor of Anglo-Saxon (Old English) at the University of Oxford. He specialized in Old and Middle English but also taught Icelandic and Finnish as well as medieval mythology. His research on *Beowulf* is still considered a standard in the field. By itself, this would make him an exemplary academic but would most likely not recommend him as the topic of a book. Tolkien, however, unlike most Oxford dons, stepped out of his role as professor to create popular literature. Or rather, he used his professorial scholarship to reach out to the public with his subject in an unusual way: by drawing upon his expansive knowledge, he created a new mythology for the modern age.

Tolkien's best-known writings were *The Hobbit* and *The Lord of the Rings*, but he also wrote other works, including *The Silmarillion*, *Father Giles of Ham*, *Mr. Bliss*, *Roverandom*, and the scholarly *The Monsters and the Critics.* In his writings, he created a fully realized world known as Middle-earth, vaguely identifiable as Northern Europe in a pre-history that never was. To bring his world to life, he produced detailed geography and cartography as well as a legendary background. He peopled the world with diverse types of inhabitants and created spoken and written languages for them. By doing this, he essentially created modern fantasy literature and a standard for subsequent writers to chase and miss. A British poll at the end of the twentieth century named *The Lord of the Rings* the most important English-language work of that century.

During his lifetime, Tolkien did not appreciate people focusing on him rather than on his writings. He felt that his writings were more worthy of attention. With apologies to the late gentleman, he is now due some notice.

Early Life

Mabel Suffield of Birmingham, England, was only eighteen years old when she received a proposal of marriage from Arthur Reuel Tolkien, who was thirteen years her senior. Because of Mabel's youth, her parents denied her their permission, but Arthur persevered over the following two years. In the end, he won her hand, but not before making some drastic changes to his prospects, which in Birmingham were quite limited. With little possibility of advancement at Lloyd's Bank, Arthur decided to try his chances in South Africa. Securing a position with the Bank of Africa, he quickly worked his way up the ladder. He eventually became a branch manager in Bloemfontein, about 650 miles northeast of Cape Town. Bloemfontein was the capital of the Orange Free State, which at the time was a sovereign Boer republic but in 1910 would become part of the Union of South Africa.

Shortly after Mabel's twenty-first birthday, she left by boat for Africa, and the couple was married in Cape Town on April 16, 1891. They then traveled by rail to Bloemfontein, where Mabel tried to make the best of her rather provincial location. Whereas Arthur loved his new country, the heat and dust from the veldt irritated Mabel, and it wasn't long before she began looking forward to home leave back in England. Very soon, however, her and Arthur's first son arrived to keep her company. John Ronald Reuel, known as Ronald in his early years, was born somewhat prematurely on January 3, 1892. A brother, Hilary Reuel, followed in February 1894.

When young Ronald became ill, his parents decided that Mabel should take the children back to England so that he could recuperate in the cooler climate. She returned to England without Arthur in April 1895 since Arthur didn't feel that he could leave his work at the time. He expressed the intent to come later, but kept procrastinating. After some months, word reached Mabel that Arthur had contracted rheumatic fever. She began making preparations to return to Bloemfontein to tend him, but Arthur developed complications and died in February 1896. He was buried alone in the Anglican cemetery, with his loved ones far away. The family never returned to South Africa.

Ronald was five when he lost his father, and by that time they had already been separated for many months. Despite his young age, he did retain a handful of strong memories of Africa, such as the time he was bitten by a tarantula. Readers of *The Hobbit* may recognize this as a source of inspiration for Bilbo's unpleasant encounter with giant spiders. Sadly, Ronald's only memory of his father was of Arthur leaning over a steamer trunk, paintbrush in hand, painting Ronald's name for identification.

With only a small income from mine stock, Mabel was now dependent upon assistance from her family. She settled herself and the boys in the tiny hamlet of Sarehole, nestled amidst a bit of old forest not far outside Birmingham. The few houses of Sarehole hugged a road along which cows were driven to market in the city. The contrast between the harsh aridity of Africa and Ronald's lush new surroundings was particularly affecting, and he learned to love the English countryside deeply. Together with his younger brother—the two of them dressed in Little Lord Fauntleroy outfits with matching long hair—Ronald blissfully roamed the nearby Warwickshire countryside, a part of the West Midlands region. Its natural beauty, complete with thick woods, Moseley Bog, two mills with millponds, and flowered meadows and dells, would remain in his memory to be tapped periodically by his muse. Tolkien's final story, "Smith of Wootton Major," was a panegyric to Sarehole, which had by then been swallowed by Birmingham. Today, however, Sarehole Mill has been restored, Tolkien's childhood house survives, and there exists a lively business in Tolkien tours.

In Sarehole, Mabel homeschooled the children. Ronald was able to read by the early age of four, and Mabel incorporated French, German, and Latin into the curriculum as well. Tolkien later credited both his love of philology and love of romance to his mother. Her curriculum also included lessons in handwriting, which was particularly stylized since the Suffield family had been engravers in generations past and the talent had survived in Mabel to be passed on to Ronald.

Mabel also included a healthy dose of fairy tales in her childrearing. One of Ronald's favorite authors was George MacDonald, a minister who wrote tales of dragons and goblins. MacDonald was a mentor to Louis Carroll, and his children's fantasies are said to have influenced writers ranging from Tolkien and C. S. Lewis to Madeleine L'Engle. By age six, Ronald was already attempting to write a poem about a green dragon.

An Eventful Year

The family was sad to leave Sarehole but had to relocate to Birmingham in 1900 so that Ronald could attend school. The difference between the bucolic countryside and the industrial pollution of Birmingham would later find expression in the differences between the Shire of Middle-earth and the evil realm of Mordor. Ronald passed his school entrance exam on the second try and was enrolled in the same grammar school that his father had attended, the elite King Edward's School. A relative helped with the tuition.

Ronald's subjects included Latin, Greek, and French. Botany was also required, which allowed him to further his love of nature. At about this time, Ronald's precocious interest in languages was spurred. He began to notice the Welsh names on railway cars coming through the train station behind his house, and he was mesmerized. In later years, he attributed his lifelong love of language to those snippets of Welsh that whet his appetite.

Another significant change took place in the spring of 1900, while the family was still living in Sarehole: Mabel converted to Catholicism. Both the Tolkien and Suffield families were stunned, and Mabel, who had relied upon her family for financial support, was now cut off. Dissatisfied with the Catholic church they attended while living in the house by the railroad tracks, she moved the family next door to the Birmingham Oratory in 1902 and became friendly with the parish priest, Father Francis Xavier Morgan. Ronald was impressed that Father Francis could speak Spanish, and he learned a bit of it with the help of Father Francis' books. Without family assistance, Mabel was not long able to afford the fees at King Edward's, so she enrolled Ronald and Hilary in Catholic school instead. The school was poor, however, and the education proved inferior, so she again began to tutor the boys at home. Ronald was eventually able to secure an academic scholarship and returned to King Edward's, where he became a student leader with a devoted circle of friends. Close male camaraderie was a pattern that would be repeated throughout his life, from grammar school to the military and finally as an Oxford don, and it would find literary expression in his Fellowship of the Ring.

Truth be told, Ronald was not the best student. He soon lost interest in the required curricular languages because the Northern languages had captured his heart. He was known as a lazy pupil because, instead of doing his schoolwork, he preferred to spend time creating languages with names like Nevbosh and Naffarin. Unlike the languages made up by most children, his were astonishing, containing advanced phonology and grammar. At the same time, he was studying the Germanic languages on his own time. This interest began with school study of Chaucer and Middle English (12th–15th centuries). He then began to teach himself Old English, or Anglo-Saxon, and learned of its relationship to Old Norse, Old High German, and the other Germanic languages. In due course, he purchased a primer of Gothic, a quite ancient Germanic language, and began what he later said was his first study of a language purely from love. Subsequently, he turned to Anglo-Saxon, Old Norse, and the Celtic languages.

Orphanhood

When Ronald was twelve, Mabel fell ill with a wasting disease. Christmastime 1903 saw her joyously anticipating Ronald's First Communion, but at the same time she was experiencing exhaustion and sleeplessness. Her condition quickly worsened, and she entered the hospital in April 1904 for what would be an extended stay. There she was diagnosed with diabetes, which in those days before insulin injections was fatal. The boys were separated and sent to live with different relatives. Mabel rallied in the summer and was able to leave the hospital. The boys were reunited with their mother, and Father Francis arranged for them to let rooms in a country cottage belonging to the Birmingham Oratory, where Mabel could convalesce. Father Francis was able to visit often, and the adult Ronald recalled how the priest would often smoke a pipe there, which he never did in the city. Ronald would wonder if his own, later pipe-smoking stemmed from that happy vacation. Mabel's recovery soon proved to be temporary, however; she fell into a diabetic coma and died in that cottage in November 1904, leaving Ronald and Hilary orphaned.

Even in his youth, Ronald was aware of the toll his mother's Catholicism had taken on her. Losing the emotional and financial support of most of her family had exhausted Mabel. Ronald viewed her as a sainted martyr to their faith and was grateful to her for leading her sons to firm religious commitment. Indeed, her dedication and resolve strengthened his own. The passing of his mother in this way colored and deepened his religious devotion forever after, but it also made him aware at an early age of the world's imperfection and its capacity for death.

In accordance with Mabel's will, Father Francis became the boys' legal guardian. The priest supplemented Mabel's bequest with subsidies from his own private funds. He established the boys in their Aunt Beatrice Suffield's boarding house. She was not as opposed to Catholicism as Mabel's other relatives were, and she cared for the boys for four years, though she was rather cold and aloof. During this time, the brothers served as altar boys and retained a close connection with the priests of the Oratory. In addition, Father Francis took the boys on annual summer vacations. Eventually, Ronald complained about his aunt's behavior—she had burned their mother's personal papers without asking—to the priest, who found the boys new lodgings.

This proved to be a fortuitous change. Ronald made the acquaintance of a fellow boarder, Edith Bratt, who was also an orphan. She was three years Ronald's senior, but the two soon formed a bond. Edith had been trained in piano and was expected to play for the landlady's soirées, but otherwise she was shunted back into her room and was not allowed to practice. Edith was unhappy, Ronald was hungry, and the two became friends over conspiracies to steal food from the kitchen.

When Father Francis became aware that the two were socializing surreptitiously outside the boarding house, he put an end—temporarily at least— to the relationship. At sixteen, Ronald was considered too young to be involved with a young lady, and the relationship could only detract from his studies. Given his financial circumstances, Ronald would be able to attend Oxford only if he won a scholarship, so he needed to spend his time studying for the qualifying exams. Further complicating the issue, the young lady in question was not Catholic. Accordingly, Ronald and Hilary were moved to other quarters.

Although Ronald understood the reasons for the enforced separation, he fell into some melancholia over the loss. What is more, Father Francis had been hurt by Ronald's sneaking around, and their relationship became strained. Edith simplified matters by finding new lodging in another town. She was happy there, able to practice piano again, and became quite actively involved at the local Anglican church, where she began to play organ. Father Francis requested that Ronald not write to her until he was twenty-one.

School Days

Meanwhile, life at King Edward's School was good. Ronald became part of a close circle of friends, initially known as the Tea Club because they snuck tea into the school library for their lively intellectual discussions. Later, they started meeting in the tearoom at Barrow's Stores and so changed their name to the Barrovian Society. Ultimately, they called themselves by the combined name of "T.C.B.S.," and they were a group devoted to youthful intellectual inquiry. Ronald was also an enthusiastic rugby player, breaking his nose on one occasion. He also belonged to other school clubs, including the debating society, where he amused his friends by opining in Latin and Greek, and even Gothic and Anglo-Saxon. In later years, he would sadly write that only one of these close friends from his grammar school days survived the Great War.

Ronald eventually succeeded in winning a small scholarship to Oxford on his second try. Had he been more interested in the subject matter, he doubtless would have performed better. Much of what Ronald learned at King Edward's came in the form of his devoted self-study of languages that were not in the curriculum.

Before entering college, Ronald took a summer mountain climbing trip to Switzerland. This was a rare occasion in which he actually traveled abroad. There is no doubt that this expedition provided material for his later writings; Bilbo's journey through the Misty Mountains was directly based upon it. A rockfall that nearly swept members of the group off a cliff made a particular impression. During the trip, Ronald happened to purchase a postcard reproduction of a German painting called *Der Berggeist* (The Mountain Spirit) by Josef Madlener. The depiction of the mountain spirit shows an old man with a long, pointed white beard, a hat with a wide, round brim, and a long red cloak. Years later, Ronald referred to this painting as the origin of Gandalf.

Upon arrival at Exeter College, Oxford, Ronald was delighted to have his own rooms at last, along with a small stipend of 60 pounds, but the subject of money continued to be a vexing one—he was usually in debt. Had he performed better on his scholarship exam, the award would have been larger. As at King Edward's, he joined a number of clubs and was lackadaisical with his required subjects. He soon became bored with the curriculum of Classics. Instead of studying, he stayed up late into the night smoking—by now he had taken up the pipe—and talking with friends, and as a result he slept late and stopped going to mass for a time. He also continued creating his own languages, and the sketching and calligraphy that he had first learned under his mother's tutelage began ripening into maturity. The one college subject Ronald truly loved was Comparative Philology—the history of words and the relationship between languages—and he was privileged to study it with the very scholar who had written the Gothic primer that first attracted Ronald to the subject years before.

In the summer of 1912, following his first year at Oxford, Ronald participated in exercises with a cavalry unit that he had joined, King Edward's Horse. He spent a wet two weeks with the regiment and resigned not long after. He did learn something useful for his later writing, however: what it was like to travel on horseback and sleep rough in a tent.

For as long as he could, Ronald delayed studying for the first series of the two major exams required for graduation in the Classics. The exams took the form of academic papers demonstrating mastery of the subject matter. Ronald produced acceptable work but again failed to excel. This led to some unforeseen consequences: the college rector suggested that Ronald make a change. Since his comparative philology paper was the only one that truly shined, why not change his area of specialty to English, which would enable him to focus on the precursor languages that he loved? In fact, it is rather surprising that no one had thought of this earlier. In 1913, then, Ronald finally arrived at the proper address for his calling. Now he was able to gain credit for what he had previously studied when he was supposed to have been studying Classics: Old English, Medieval English, and the Germanic languages. A special area of study was Old Norse, with its epics, sagas, and myths, which thoroughly captured his fancy.

Edith

On January 3, 1913, Ronald turned twenty-one, and he immediately wrote to Edith Bratt with a declaration of love and proposal of marriage. He was dismayed to hear in reply that she was engaged to someone else! Edith's letter, however, was gentle. She explained how she had come to doubt that Ronald would still be interested in resuming their relationship. She had only accepted the other young man because he was kind and she had to look to her future.

With such equivocation from Edith, there was only one thing Ronald could do: he traveled to Cheltenham to win her back. It didn't take long; by the end of the day, she had agreed to marry him.

Yet the issue of Edith's religion remained. Ronald sought her whole-hearted devotion to the Catholic Church. Edith committed to a Catholic conversion, but separation from the Anglican Church would be hard for her: she was by now very socially involved in it. Writing to Father Francis of the engagement, Ronald feared a toxic response. Instead, Father Francis made an attempt to be supportive. On the other hand, anti-Catholic sentiment was very strong in some quarters of England at the time. When Edith informed the couple with whom she lodged of her intention to convert, she was told to find other housing. She would eventually find lodging with her cousin Jenny Grove, who would remain her companion throughout Edith's and Ronald's wartime wanderings. Ronald saw in Edith's trials an echo of his mother's, which could only have elevated Edith still more in his eyes. Still, the course of true love was not without its hiccups. After three years apart, the couple would have to relearn their closeness. The process came at the cost of some annoyance and compromise.

From our contemporary standpoint, the amount of time the couple now spent apart seems unusual. Ronald was in no hurry to tell his college and T.C.B.S. friends about his engagement, and Edith remained separate from the male-dominated life of his academic career. Moreover, Ronald spent much of his summer vacation time traveling without her. The summer of 1913 found him engaged as the escort of two Mexican boys traveling to Paris. They were joined by a third boy and two aunts in Paris. Ronald's charges then decided to make a side trip to Brittany, where a rather traumatizing event occurred: one of the aunts was run over by a car while out walking. Ronald helped transport her back to the hotel, where she died within hours. He then undertook the terrible task of having the body shipped back to Mexico and accompanying the grieving boys back to England. Ronald had disliked France and the French to begin with, and one can't help but wonder if this entire unpleasant experience lay behind his limited foreign travel thereafter.

Exactly one year to the day after his reunion with Edith—January 8, 1914—Edith was welcomed into the Catholic Church. The young couple's engagement was formally announced in church shortly thereafter.

Ronald continued to lead a busy and challenging life in Oxford. He played tennis, punted (a type of inland boating with a pole), and became president of the college debating society. There were also many friends with whom to meet for dinner and social activities.

Edith, on the other hand, found her new Catholic life to be tedious. Loss of her Anglican social life left her virtually friendless. She was now living with a cousin in their own house in Warwick, where the available Catholic church was less than exciting and had no need of Edith's organ-playing services. As a result, her early enthusiasm for church attendance quickly dwindled.

The Great War

The summer of 1914 found Ronald vacationing in Cornwall with a priest of the Birmingham Oratory. This was followed by a brief visit to his Aunt Jane's farm, where his brother Hilary, who had left school, was working. On a larger stage, events were not so bucolic. Archduke Franz Ferdinand of Austria, heir to the Austro-Hungarian throne, and his wife Sophie were assassinated on June 28, 1914. A crisis involving most of the countries in Europe ensued, based on a complicated series of treaties and rivalries. War broke out, with Britain entering the fray on August 4. Because there was no mandatory conscription until January 1916, it was only government censorship and misdirection that fanned patriotism and led vast numbers of young men to enlist and create the largest volunteer army in British history. The subsequent war losses proved catastrophic. Tragically, at least 700,000 British soldiers died, but the figures may have been even higher.

Ronald, however, had other ideas. As an orphan, he needed—more than most—to safeguard his future career. He was determined to complete his degree. College life now became dismal because his friends had all enlisted. He found off-campus rooms with the one good friend who remained behind due to ill health. He also signed up for the Officer's Training Corps, which would allow him to continue his studies while training for the army.

Ronald passed his final exams with highest honors in 1915, assuring him a future academic career—if he survived the war. It was now time to face army life, and he assumed his commission as a second lieutenant. The four closest members of the T.C.B.S. were all immersed in the military now. Their letters and records of rare meetings indicate the extent to which they clung to their friendship and idealism in wartime. The four believed themselves capable of doing great things, both collectively and individually, for society. Now it was an open question whether any of them would survive, a reality of which they were all becoming increasingly aware. Of Ronald's T.C.B.S. friends, in the end only Christopher Wiseman, for whom Ronald's third son was named, survived.

Ronald's next six months were spent in dreary tedium. He abhorred the bureaucracy of the military and the repetitive style of training. Eventually, he decided to undergo training in "signaling," which included Morse and other codes, making it a natural specialization for a linguist. He learned to use semaphore flags and to handle carrier pigeons. When the time came to utilize what he had learned, however, the chaos of the battlefield meant that, most of the time, it would be necessary to rely upon runners. This no doubt influenced the way he later described message-taking and the use of winged creatures in his novels. As a signaler, Ronald also learned map reading, which would be useful in the later creation of maps of Middle-earth. Apart from being more interesting than other work of the infantry, signaling would increase his chances for survival in the trenches, although it's not certain whether that was a consideration for him when he selected it. Nevertheless, as a signaler, he wouldn't be leading any assaults on the enemy lines. In his spare time, Ronald continued reading Icelandic, writing poetry, and doggedly maintaining his interests and his work to the extent possible.

In his poem "The Wanderer's Allegiance," written in March 1916, Ronald confessed awareness of how insular his life had been. In it, he shared how his happy dreams had kept him from hearing "the world's distress." Like other young men, however, his time in the military was expanding his contacts and experiences—sometimes in the worst possible way— beyond his otherwise sheltered life. In the army, he was learning to endure in conditions of intense physical discomfort, and he was encountering types of people he would not ordinarily have met. British society at the time was strongly divided by class, but the war was bringing all types into close association. Although Ronald was unimpressed with his superiors, he was surprised by the decency of the common private. As an officer, he had his own "batman," a personal attendant who performed domestic duties but also served as a runner for his officer during action. The simple, honest, and devoted character of Samwise Gamgee would later be fashioned out of the virtuous "Tommies" that Ronald met during the Great War.

By this time, it was no longer possible to conceal the horrifying numbers of young Englishmen being killed at the front. Ronald and Edith decided to marry before his departure, knowing full well that he might not return. At the end of March 1916, they were married by Father Francis at the church in Warwick. Since the marriage occurred during Lent, there was no Nuptial Mass, although the couple was able to enjoy a week's honeymoon. Edith took rooms near Ronald's base, but at the beginning of June, he shipped off to France. He had no great expectation of survival.

Before Ronald left, he and Edith devised a code so that Edith could know where he was in France. At the time, soldiers' mail was being heavily censored to prevent letter writers from revealing anything about troop movements. There was a fear that such letters could be intercepted by the enemy. Whole swathes of a letter would consequently be either blacked out or cut out by the military censors. To circumvent this restriction, Ronald would include a series of dots in his letters to reveal to Edith his location, and this way they could share a secret and feel close across the miles.

At first, Ronald spent time at a base camp, but three weeks after arriving in France, Ronald's battalion embarked by train for the Somme, an area in northern France that was the site of some of the bloodiest battles of the war. They arrived in time for the worst of those battles, the Somme Offensive of 1916.

Luckily for Tolkien, his battalion was held back, billeted in a hamlet while row after row of advancing British and French soldiers were gunned down as they climbed out of the trenches and marched across the open space of no-man's land. The battle would continue from July 1 until November 18, during which time an estimated one million men were killed or wounded. On the first day alone, July 1, 1916, some 20,000 British were killed and 40,000 wounded. It is considered the worst day in the history of the British army, and since the losses were especially catastrophic among the enthusiastic volunteers known as Kitchener's Army, the pain cut across all of British society. Among the dead was aspiring artist Rob Gilson, one of Ronald's closest friends from the T.C.B.S. and the son of the headmaster of St. Edward's. He had been killed while fatalistically leading a charge of his platoon across no-man's land.

Ronald would thankfully miss that horrific day; not until July 15 would his company enter the battle. His time alternated between the mud and horror of the trenches and resting in a billet. By July 21, he was made battalion signal officer, which was becoming a near-impossible job given the unreliability of telephone wires that could be blown up or tapped and early Morse code transmissions that could be overheard through the ground across no-man's land. Visual signals drew enemy fire, the Germans were intercepting key orders, and it was unclear how messages could be sent safely.

When he was able, Ronald attended Mass. Occasionally, he was able to meet and commiserate with another of his T.C.B.S. friends, G. B. Smith, the poet of the group and the T.C.B.S. member with whom Ronald was closest. In December, Smith would succumb to gas gangrene caused by light shrapnel wounds, but by that time Tolkien was no longer in the trenches. Like so many others, Ronald had contracted "trench fever," a persistent high fever that was later discovered to have been spread by lice. This malady probably saved his life when so many in his battalion were killed. At the beginning of November, five months after arriving in France, Ronald was evacuated back to England, where he would spend the rest of the war in and out of hospitals.

Smith found comfort in the knowledge that Ronald was safely back home. In a letter sent some months before his fatal injuries, Smith wrote to Ronald that the spirit of the T.C.B.S. would carry on in him. He tragically asked his friend to give voice to what they had dreamed together. With the loss of his T.C.B.S. friends, Tolkien, for his part, felt that something in the world had been broken.

Myth Making

Tolkien's efforts as a writer occurred firmly within his training and interests as a philologist. The late-18th- and 19th-century rediscovery of European fairy and folk tales was closely allied with the development of philology as a science. The brothers Grimm, for example, created a historical dictionary of German based on their forays into German folklore. The tales compiled by Andrew Lang in his colored fairy books brought such literature to English children, and Tolkien was influenced by them at his mother's knee.

For some time, Ronald had been trying his hand at original creations in both poetry and prose. At university, his interests began to converge as he took his first tentative steps toward creating a unified mythology. As might be expected, Tolkien's first inspiration in this regard came from the existing mythology that he was reading. In particular, Ronald was fascinated by a 9th-century poem by the Anglo-Saxon poet Cynewulf, whose religious poem *Christ* included the Old English word for the known inhabited world: *middangeard*, translated as "Middle-earth." The poem makes reference to a being called Earendal, who is the brightest of angels above Middle-earth and is sent to humans. Within the context of the Christian poem, Earendal is understood as John the Baptist, but it is believed that an older astrological myth underlies this usage. In the earlier layer of myth, Earendal would have been the morning star, herald of the rising sun. Ronald found the reference in the poem to be unusually powerful, and it percolated in his imagination for some time. Then, while visiting on his aunt's farm in that summer of 1914 and following his vacation at the sea in Cornwall, he wrote a poem entitled, "The Voyage of Eärendel the Evening Star." In it, he describes how Earendal's ship leaps from the sea into the sky and journeys across the heavens.

At the same time Ronald was endeavoring to create literature, he continued working to create his own, personal language. The one he was developing at that time was heavily influenced by Finnish and would eventually develop into Quenya, the High Elven language in *The Lord of the Rings*. As the elements of his creativity began to come together, Ronald decided that a language needed a history and a literature. It needed a people who spoke it. He decided upon the faerie folk that Earendal met while his ship was still on its earthly travels. To elaborate this notion, he wrote "The Lay of Earendal." Although his ideas would evolve considerably over time, he was now forging the path his future work would take. Meanwhile, however, war intervened, and this undoubtedly brought a darker cast to his subsequent work than would have been the case otherwise. In other ways, however, Tolkien refused to have his course altered despite the dramatic cultural shifts then taking place. The T.C.B.S. had dreamed great things, and Ronald felt charged to be its torchbearer.

Tolkien repeatedly denied that the war had any impact on his writing, but his later friend C. S. Lewis had no doubt that it was otherwise. Lewis, who had shared the experience of war with the other young men of his generation, wrote of how Tolkien captured the eerie silence before a battle, the camaraderie and shared moral support of the soldiers, and the joy of basic comforts, such as finding an unexpected bit of tobacco.

Certainly, the Great War forever changed those who participated. For better or worse, the world of the past, its institutions and aristocracies, was left in rubble, leaving widespread, bitter disillusionment. It is no surprise then that literary style also underwent radical changes. Writers of that generation were repulsed by the traditional, drum-beating way of reporting the war. They understood the extent to which empty words about heroism and grandeur had cloaked the sheer carnage. Simply put they had been lied to. These young writers viewed the manners and elegance of past writing as deceitful distortions. Their new style of modernism had no patience for evasion from the truth: it could be brutal in its succinctness.

Not so Tolkien, however. He emerged as a solitary voice insistent upon salvaging what was worthwhile, and he saw much that was valuable. Anyone versed in myth understands the extent to which it pivots on the human condition and particularly the theme of death. This made it eminently suitable for expressing the real-life experience and ruminations of a returning soldier. Increasingly, his poems— like "The Fall of Gondolin," written while recuperating from trench fever—were no longer solitary creations, but rather were mapping out an interconnected mythic web of "lost tales." (These "lost tales," as he called them, would be edited and published posthumously as *The Silmarillion* by his son Christopher.)

Tolkien was not the first to resurrect myth as a genre for contemporary writing. He had read the works of William Morris during the time of his engagement to Edith, and these writings influenced him in very specific ways, a fact he freely admitted in late-life correspondence. Morris had preceded Tolkien at Exeter to become one of the most influential figures of 19th-century British culture. The guiding light of the Arts and Crafts movement, his literary accomplishments are lesser known today, yet his *A Tale of the House of the Wolfings* is considered a precursor to current fantasy literature.

As with Tolkien, Morris's writing was heavily influenced by legendary Norwegian and Icelandic sources. Morris's love of nature, well known from his fabulous textile designs, was represented in his writings with detailed descriptions of the natural setting, a feature Tolkien would emulate. Tolkien would also borrow from Morris the name Mirkwood, the frequent use of Germanic names and archaic words, and the idea of dwarves as talented smiths. Most important, however, was the effort to create a new mythology for England that would speak to the modern reader.

The End of the War

Following his recovery from fever, Tolkien was left weak, emaciated, and unfit for duty. The fever recurred several times. He was eventually placed on light duty, mostly keeping watch over the sea, but again fell victim to fever. Edith, meanwhile, was expecting their first child. Having moved more than twenty times in only a few years, she was determined to have the child in Cheltenham, even though Ronald was stationed in Hull. On November 16, 1917, John Francis Reuel was born. The "Francis" was for Father Francis while "Reuel" had been Ronald's father's middle name and was his and his brother Hilary's as well. The name means "friend of God" in Hebrew, and he esteemed it so highly that he would pass it on as a middle name to all his eventual four children. John's birth left Edith in critical condition. A week later, Ronald was able to obtain leave and was present with a recovering Edith when Father Francis baptized the child.

Edith moved with the baby to Roos, in Yorkshire, to be close to Ronald. They were able to see each other whenever he obtained leave. On one occasion, they went for a walk in the woods, where Edith sang and danced, looking more beautiful than ever before to him. From that incident came a new story for his envisioned book of lost tales: a tale of the human Beren, who falls in love with the elf Tinúviel—the name was later changed to Lúthien—when he sees her dancing in the woods. The story would develop over time as a pivotal piece of *The Silmarillion* and be briefly retold by Aragorn in *The Lord of the Rings.*

In April 1918, Ronald was found fit for battle, but by the time the order came at the end of July, he had contracted gastritis and was once again in the hospital. By that time, the battalion with which he had fought in France had been all but obliterated. It was, in fact, disbanded in August. Instead of returning to the front, Ronald spent the rest of the war, which ended on November 11, in the hospital.

With the end of the war, Tolkien returned with Edith to an Oxford depleted of its youth. So many of his friends were now dead. The sadness of loss would remain with him throughout his life.

The Linguist at Work

When Tolkien returned to Oxford, it was a university largely without students. The university could not hire him under such uncertain circumstances. Luckily for Tolkien, his former teacher of Old Norse, William Craigie, was now one of four editors of the original, not yet completed *Oxford English Dictionary* (then known as the *New English Dictionary*) and hired him as an assistant lexicographer. The dictionary was meant to be the most thorough and complete dictionary of the English language to date; work on it had been going on for over sixty years. It would finally be completed in 1928, when the first copies of the prestigious work would be presented to King George V and President Calvin Coolidge.

Tolkien would spend 1919 and 1920 investigating the origin, history, and pronunciation of specific entries beginning with the letter W. He worked on such words as *waggle, waistcoat,* and *walrus,* looking for every historical use of the words that he could locate and tracing how the meanings had changed. Years later he stated that he learned more in those two years than he had during any other period of his education. His supervising editor was the autodidact Henry Bradley, who found Tolkien to be exceptionally competent and erudite. Tolkien later offered a tongue-in-cheek look at the work of compiling dictionaries in *Farmer Giles of Ham*, where he advised checking for word meanings with the "four wise clerks of Oxenford." Late in life, in 1970, Tolkien would be asked to provide one final definition for the dictionary—for the word *hobbit*.

In 1919, Tolkien was presented with a master's degree from Oxford, an honorary degree automatically granted for having been in residence five years. While working on the dictionary, he also began privately tutoring students from Oxford. The British learning system required that students attend lectures but also receive one-on-one training from tutors. As a result, Tolkien's income was sufficient that he and Edith were able to move to a small house where, in 1920, their second child, Michael Hilary Reuel, was born. Eventually, Tolkien had a sufficient number of students to enable him to resign his position with the dictionary. Shortly thereafter, he obtained a position as "reader" (a lower rank than professor) in English at the University of Leeds, and Edith and the two children followed a few months later. He was named a professor in 1924 at the age of thirty-two, making him the youngest professor at the university.

Leeds was a manufacturing city located halfway between London and Scotland. With its terrible industrialized pollution, it represented much of what Tolkien disliked about the modern world. Coal grime from the coal-fired factories caused him to change his detachable shirt collars multiple times a day. Nevertheless, he did find things to appreciate in his new environment. If the students weren't as bright as those at Oxford, he was impressed with how tenaciously they worked. They brought a commitment to their studies that he had not always found at Oxford. Tolkien also enjoyed the opportunity to hear the local West Yorkshire dialect.

Otherwise, Tolkien was likely too busy to dwell much on the negative side of the situation. His teaching schedule was rigorous. The courses he taught while at Leeds included Old and Middle English texts, Old and Middle English philology, the history of English, introductory German philology, Gothic, Old Icelandic, and Medieval Welsh. In effect, he was teaching Northern myths and legends under the all-important rubric of language instruction. The two facets, in his mind, were always indivisible.

While his interlude at Leeds was relatively brief, lasting only from 1920 to 1925, it resulted in a fruitful academic collaboration. A former pupil of Tolkien at Oxford, E.V. Gordon, arrived at Leeds as a lecturer in the English Department, and the two became great friends. Together with his new colleague, Tolkien prepared an edition of *Sir Gawain and the Green Knight* (published in 1925 by Clarendon Press).

There was at the time no edition of this Middle English poem appropriate for university study. Tolkien prepared the translation of the text and a scholarly glossary while Gordon undertook most of the notes. In a more whimsical collaboration, the two formed the Viking Society, a club for Leeds students that was devoted to drinking beer, reading Old Icelandic sagas, and singing ridiculous songs in Anglo-Saxon, mostly written by Tolkien or Gordon. Like so many of Tolkien's associates, Gordon died young, thereby ending a productive collaboration for him. By that time, however, Tolkien had moved on to Oxford.

During this happy time, Tolkien was also writing poems for his mythology, including "The Dragon's Visit," which included a character called "Miss Baggins," and "Glip," about an unnatural creature with glowing eyes who lives under the floor of a cave. At one point, the family received a visit from Tolkien's cantankerous grandfather, John Suffield. Suffield otherwise spent most of his time living in Worcestershire with his daughter, Tolkien's Aunt Jane, who at the time was residing on a farm known to the locals as "Bag End." This was a name Tolkien would later borrow for the hobbit abode of Mr. Bilbo Baggins. Clearly, Tolkien's imagination at this time was percolating with many ideas that would soon come to fruition.

The Coalbiters and the Inklings

In 1925 Tolkien returned to Oxford as Rawlinson and Bosworth Professor of Anglo-Saxon, a position he held until 1945, when he was named Merton Professor of English Language and Literature. The position he assumed when he came to Oxford was in fact William Craigie's position. Craigie had resigned in order to go to America to compose a new American dictionary. Tolkien settled into a decades-long routine as an Oxford professor.

As at Leeds, Tolkien founded an informal club at Oxford for reading and discussing Norse sagas. This was not, after all, literature that was written to be read silently; it was intended for oral recitation, which needs an audience. The club was known as the Coalbiters, a name derived from an Icelandic term for someone who stays so close to the fire in winter that he "bites coal." In effect, it was the latest incarnation of the T.C.B.S. This time, the members were mostly Oxford faculty. An early, important member of the Coalbiters was C. S. Lewis.

C. S. Lewis, the author of the *Chronicles of Narnia*, joined the faculty at Oxford as a fellow at Magdalen College and tutor in English language and literature at about the same time Tolkien moved from Leeds to Oxford. Lewis was known to his friends as Jack. When he first joined the Coalbiters, Lewis did not know Old Icelandic, but the sagas had always fascinated him, and thus began the close association of Tolkien and Lewis. They shared quick minds and a scorn for modernism. After meetings, the two would often talk late into the night. In addition, Tolkien and Lewis began to schedule regular meetings in which they would traverse the gamut of intellectual discourse.

Once the targeted sagas had been read, the Coalbiters segued into another group, the Inklings, which began life as a literary club organized by an undergraduate. Because the student wanted continuity in the group, he asked some dons to become members. Within a couple of years, the student element had petered out, leaving the club consisting solely of adult professionals, not all of whom were academics. Membership in the group was informal and varied somewhat over time, but without question the club's core driving force was Lewis, assisted by his beloved brother, "Warnie" (Warren), a retired military officer. This adult version of the Inklings started in in 1933. Throughout the 1930s and 1940s, the group met regularly on Thursday evenings in Lewis's rooms at Magdalen College and also before lunch on Tuesdays in a local pub, The Eagle and Child (known affectionately as The Bird and Baby). The Thursday night meetings in particular comprised members sharing their work-in-progress writings. *The Hobbit* was largely completed before the group was organized, but Tolkien eventually shared chapters of *The Lord of the Rings* with the Inklings. Their criticism, especially that of Lewis, compelled him to better writing and, perhaps more importantly, to the continuation and completion of his writing. He dedicated the first edition of *The Lord of the Rings* to the Inklings.

Tolkien and Lewis were friends for twenty-five years despite representing opposite sides of the Oxford English School faculty. At the time, the Oxford English School was newly formed as a separate faculty and still finding its way. Lewis represented the literature side of English study, Tolkien the philological. To begin with, Tolkien and Lewis were actually quite suspicious and wary of one another because of this difference, but before long their mutual interest in writing, mythology, and religion drew them together. With Lewis' help, Tolkien was able to push through his agenda of creating new requirements for English majors (the English School syllabus) that united the previously opposing sides of the Oxford English faculty. Tolkien believed doggedly in the old-fashioned notion that the purpose of philology was to read literature and that literature couldn't be properly studied without philology. Tolkien did not consider himself to be well read in English literature, per se; it didn't interest him. It had always been the form and shape of words that intrigued him.

Consequently, it was literature in foreign languages—mostly precursors of English—that drew him. Accordingly, the emphasis in the syllabus would be put on medieval English, and in fact the syllabus would stop with the Victorian Age at approximately 1830 because, in Tolkien's and Lewis's opinion, students could understand literature at that point on their own and didn't need coursework in it. Oxford would revisit that position as early as the 1950s.

At one point, as a lark, Tolkien and Lewis both agreed to write a piece of science fiction. The year was 1936, and Lewis was bemoaning a dearth of the kind of literature they both enjoyed. He challenged Tolkien to create some, and Tolkien reminded his friend of a similar wager between Lord Byron and the Shelleys that had led Mary Shelley to produce *Frankenstein.* Tolkien never finished *The Lost Road*, his resulting book about time travel. It featured a pre-*Lord of the Rings* Sauron working evil at the close of the First Age of Middle-earth. Lewis, however, completed and published *Out of the Silent Planet* (1938), which was about space travel. Tolkien communicated with his own publisher, Stanley Unwin, about Lewis' book. In his letter to Unwin, Tolkien mentioned that the story had been read serially to the Inklings and had riveted their attention. Unwin eventually referred the book to a different publisher. Tolkien would abandon *The Lost*

Road to begin work on the sequel to the Hobbit, which would later become *The Lord of the Rings*.

It was largely Tolkien's influence that spurred Lewis on during the last stage of his conversion from atheism to the Christian faith. Lewis had in fact been searching for a satisfying philosophy for years and regularly engaged in intense discussions about belief with his various intellectual contacts. By 1929 he had decided that some kind of God did exist, and he had begun to attend weekday chapel and Sunday church. He was also reading the Gospel of John in Greek. Clearly, he was a man in search of his faith, although in the end he claimed that his faith had come in search of him.

Tolkien and Lewis had been debating the subject of Christian belief for some time, but one night in September 1931 convinced Lewis fully. A mutual friend and fellow Inkling, Henry Victor Dyson, known generally as Hugo Dyson, was the third active participant in the discussion that night. The conversation that evening revolved around the widely found myth of a dying god. The friends spoke long that night, with Tolkien arguing that God was the master storyteller who had created the perfect story. The implication of Tolkien's position was that all storytelling, including his own, shared in God's divine storytelling and was therefore a pathway and a signpost to the Gospel, the truest version of the dying god myth.

For his part, Tolkien was deeply grateful to Lewis for the encouragement that kept him writing. A key reason for Tolkien's indebtedness was that he had long considered his mythology to be his own private nonsense. Lewis was the first person to indicate that it deserved broad readership and should be more than a secret pastime. Tolkien was far too stubborn to change much of his writing under the sway of anyone's criticism, but the group readings helped to keep him on track; as long as he was able to share his writings with the Inklings, he made good progress. It was eventually Hugo Dyson who kept Tolkien from continuing this practice. Dyson was not a fan of Tolkien's writing and had grown tired of hearing it. He preferred the meetings to consist of lively conversation rather than more of Tolkien's hobbits. Accordingly, sometime in 1947 he began to exercise veto power in the group to keep Tolkien from sharing his work. Since it was Tolkien who at that point most frequently needed and sought out the forum as a sounding board, Dyson's action led to the slow disintegration of the Inklings as a reading group. One Thursday night in October 1949, Warnie and Lewis waited expectantly in Lewis's rooms, but no one showed up for the meeting. That was the effective end of the group, although Lewis and various friends still met less formally at pubs on Mondays or Tuesdays for the remainder of Lewis's life.

Tolkien wrote that, from around 1927 until 1940, Lewis was his closest friend and remained dear to him even afterward. Over time, however, their great friendship would cool. By the time of Lewis' death, Tolkien would write that he hadn't been one of Lewis' intimates for a decade. There were several reasons why this occurred. First, the nature of their faith was really quite different. Despite all they had in common, Tolkien was profoundly disappointed that Lewis chose the Church of England over Catholicism. He wrote that Lewis had entered Christianity through his habitual old door (the Irish-style Anglicanism into which he had been born) rather than finding a new (Catholic) one. In addition, Tolkien was unimpressed with his friend's popular theology, believing that such delving should be left to the clergy, whose job it was, rather than an upstart newcomer to the faith. He also viewed Lewis's Narnia books as slap-dash and superficially conceived.

There was also the issue of Charles Williams, with whom Lewis was quite entranced. Williams was another significant figure in the development of Christian fiction. In addition to poetry, he wrote what T. S. Eliot called "supernatural thrillers," which involved supernatural incursions into the contemporary world. He is considered a precursor for the dark supernatural genre popular today. As an editor at Oxford Press, Williams happened to be reading the proofs of Lewis's *The Allegory of Love* at the same time in 1936 that Lewis had come upon Williams's *The Place of the Lion*. Both Lewis and Williams were so taken with each other's work that they independently and nearly simultaneously penned personal letters of praise to each other. Lewis, sensing a kindred spirit, invited Williams from London to a meeting of the Inklings. In 1939, when Williams was evacuated from London with the rest of the Oxford Press, he became a regular member of the Inklings.

Williams was not physically imposing, but he was an intellectually charismatic figure with a number of adherents during his lifetime. Strikingly, his disciples included more women than was the case with either Lewis or Tolkien. Tolkien was appreciative of Williams's interest in his hobbits, but he in turn found this new member's writing to be incomprehensible (he was not alone in this assessment). More significantly, he disapproved of Williams's influence over Lewis' writing. He was leery of Williams's occultism and probably jealous of Lewis' fascination with him, for time spent under the influence of Williams was time spent growing distant from Tolkien's own affinities. Lewis was evidently aware of this tension. He claimed in his book *The Four Loves* that, within a friendship circle, growing acquaintance with a new friend does not damage an earlier friendship but rather brings broader experience of that earlier friend. Tolkien was unconvinced, however. Williams died prematurely at the age of fifty-eight, just as World War II was ending. The members of the Inklings were absolutely stunned and deeply saddened by the sudden death of Williams following abdominal surgery, and Warnie Lewis wrote in his diary that the Inklings would never be the same.

After the tragedy, Tolkien reassumed his key position among the Inklings. New members joined, including young Christopher Tolkien, who was only twenty-one but closely involved in his father's writing of *The Lord of the Rings*. Christopher would read his father's new chapters, and the Inklings preferred his renditions to those of Tolkien. Normal life resumed in the post-war period, and Tolkien took a brief vacation with the Lewis brothers.

At a crucial point in Lewis's life, Tolkien intervened. The situation had to do with Lewis's status at Oxford. Tolkien had always been concerned about his friend's somewhat insecure position there. Lewis had never been fully appreciated at

Oxford, and while his academic output was prolific, his notoriety came from writings outside his field, as a literary historian and critic. This did not earn him much academic appreciation, and he was repeatedly passed over for advancement to a professorial chair. Finally, in 1954, he was offered a new chair in Medieval and Renaissance Literature at Cambridge but turned it down, in part because he had advised someone else to apply for it. It was Tolkien who convinced him to reconsider. Once this was accomplished and Lewis ensconced at Cambridge, the two seldom saw each other, even though Lewis continued to maintain his home outside of Oxford with Warnie and to live there on weekends and off-term.

Probably the most difficult blow to their friendship was Lewis's relationship with American divorcee Helen Joy Davidman Gresham. Lewis had begun corresponding with her in 1950, and she came to England to meet him in 1952. As a Catholic, Tolkien's faith found its bedrock in the sacraments. He strongly disapproved of divorce and could not support Lewis's more liberal views on the subject, nor his eventual marriage to Joy. That marriage began with a civil ceremony in 1956 as a matter of convenience to allow Joy to remain legally in England, but it was followed by a religious ceremony after their arrangement had deepened into love. In fact, knowing how he would feel, Lewis failed to tell Tolkien about the marriage until it was a fait accompli, paralleling Tolkien's concealment of his own impending marriage from his mentor, Father Francis. By then, Lewis and Tolkien weren't seeing very much of each other, although other Oxford friends were well aware of the marriage.

Joy had been diagnosed with terminal cancer by the time of their religious ceremony, which took place at her hospital bed. It was expected that she had very little time left and would be going to Lewis's home outside Oxford to die. Instead, she went into remission, and she and Lewis had a few brief years to enjoy married life before the cancer returned.

Matters between Lewis and Tolkien then took a slightly different turn because of their wives. Edith and Lewis had never gotten along. The normally ebullient, even overbearing Lewis became tongue-tied in her presence. He seemed to have no interest in her as a person. And Lewis had no problem dragging his various friends away from their wives for lengthy evenings out. Edith had every right to resent Lewis for taking up so much of her husband's time. But on one occasion in 1960, Edith and Joy found themselves both patients in the same hospital. Joy was there for treatment of her cancer, and Edith for arthritis. Edith and Tolkien were able to meet Joy for the first time. As it happened, Edith and Joy liked each other, and that meeting helped to soften the strain between the Tolkiens and Lewises. Joy died two months later.

Lewis's health did not long outlast her. Tolkien visited the ailing Lewis, accompanied by his son, Father John, only a few weeks before Lewis's death. When Lewis died on November 22, 1963, just shy of his sixty-fifth birthday and on the same day as the Kennedy assassination, Tolkien declined to write an obituary for him. He did, however, attend the funeral and had a Catholic Mass said for his old friend. Several years later, he wrote that he still could not grasp the reality of his friend's death.

Children's Stories

Tolkien devotedly helped to rear his growing family on a somewhat meager income, but the needs of his family were difficult to juggle with his academic life. For years he had graded examination papers for the extra pay it provided, exacerbating an already overburdened work schedule. The trouble was, it was only at the end of the nineteenth century that Oxford faculty were even allowed to marry, and the lifestyle was not well suited to the married life. Dons were expected to attend chapel at 8 a.m. and then eat breakfast together. Tutorials ran from 9 until 1, and lectures and research filled the afternoon. Dinner was at 7:15. Students often met after dinner to continue their discussions. Accordingly, Edith was forced to suffer her husband's habitual absence.

Tolkien made the best of the situation by not living in his campus rooms. He met students in his home as often as possible in order to spend more time with his family. As orphans, the parents' commitment to their children ran deep. The father made certain that he was always home for lunch and tea. The children were given free admission to his study as long as he wasn't teaching there. Even so, it was necessary to race back and forth between campus and home several times a day. Wearing the traditional black robes of the Oxford don, he made the circuit on a high-seated bicycle.

More children had come in due course. A third son, Christopher John Reuel, arrived at Leeds in 1924, and Edith's wished-for daughter, Priscilla Anne Reuel, finally came in 1929. Tolkien fell into the pleasant habit of writing stories for the children. This practice had begun in 1920, when John was only three and Tolkien had started the tradition of sending a letter from Father Christmas. Each year for twenty years, the children received an illustrated letter from the North Pole relating the various amusing incidents that befell Father Christmas and his associates.

Then, too, there were the wonderful nightly stories requested by the children. Stories about elves and dwarves were favorites. Tom Bombadil stemmed from Michael Tolkien's brightly colored Dutch doll on a shelf. As he evolved, Tom Bombadil came to represent for Tolkien the spirit of the vanishing English countryside. For Michael in particular, there was a story about treelike beings because Michael shared his father's love of trees. At the time of his father's death, Michael recalled how funny and exciting the stories were, far better than the books available. Michael believed it was their realism that made them so special; Tolkien made listeners feel that they were inside the story. It was this quality in his books that made him so appreciated by countless readers. Sadly, Tolkien didn't write down most of these bedtime tales, but they aided him down the path of fiction and fantasy.

In this way grew his tale about a hobbit, which his sons recalled first hearing about as bedtime stories toward the end of the 1920s. Eventually, the oral stories would take form as a written work. The whole was not originally part of his larger mythology but over time came to be drawn into it. According to Tolkien, he first began to write down the book while grading those dreaded exam papers with which he supplemented his modest income. As anyone who has graded exams knows, the task becomes quite tedious after a while. Tolkien was engaged in this mind-numbing exercise when he was unexpectedly confronted with a blank page in an exam book. Staring at the blank page, he suddenly wrote down the first line of what would become *The Hobbit.*

When he got down to composition in earnest, he began with the names that he had selected, although he not infrequently changed them before he was done. These names served to spark his imagination. The name Bilbo, for instance, came from a thin sword from Bilbao, Spain that Tolkien owned, and as such Bilbo's small sword receives very specific mention in the book. The character of Bilbo had in actuality started out as "Bingo" before the name was finally settled.

Tolkien probably began writing in earnest in 1930, and he first showed it to Lewis in late 1932. Lewis was nearly rapturous and encouraged "Tollers," as he called his friend, to complete the work. The tale began with the tone of a story told to children but, by its ending, had grown more sophisticated and foreshadowed the darker, more mature tale to come. Tolkien dedicated *The Hobbit* to his children, but it was ultimately Lewis who had pushed him to complete it. The prestigious British publisher George Allen & Unwin (which merged in 1990 with HarperCollins) showed interest in Tolkien's story for children in 1936. As was his practice with children's literature, Sir Stanley Unwin handed the book over to his ten-year-old son, Rayner Unwin, who was asked to judge the manuscript. It passed merit, and *The Hobbit* was published with Tolkien's own illustrations in September 1937. When it was well received, the publisher asked for a sequel.

While nursery tales came easily to Tolkien, books did not. There was something about putting his thoughts and oral material into final, written form that defied him throughout his career. *The Hobbit* took about eight years to complete. During the twelve years that it took Tolkien to write *The Lord of the Rings*, Lewis undertook and completed a vast body of work, including his seven Narnia books. Tolkien never did finish *The Silmarillion* (his book of lost tales), despite working on it for fifty years. At the point when his publisher asked for a sequel to *The Hobbit*, Tolkien had been tinkering with this book of lost tales for years, revising it again and again with too perfect an eye for the incomplete. He viewed it as his most important work, the web of myths he had strived for so long to develop. Now, he turned it over to his publisher, but the reviewer could not make heads or tails of the eclectic work that, with its plethora of made-up languages, boasted no central storyline or narrator. The manuscript was returned to Tolkien as unpublishable. Consequently, he began work on a different book, one that would become *The Lord of the Rings*. *The Silmarillion* would not be published until after his death; his son Christopher would finish the task for him.

The Road to Mordor

Prior to World War II, in 1938, a German publisher was preparing to release a German-language version of *The Hobbit* and sent Tolkien a letter of inquiry asking him to validate his Aryan origins. In fact, the name "Tolkien" is believed to be German. The family seems to have had its roots in Saxony (modern-day Germany) but had been in England since the 18th century, when it became fervently English. As a matter of fact, while he was a boy at King Edward's School, young Ronald had helped line the route for the coronation parade of King George V. Still, Tolkien could easily have fallen back upon his father's Germanic ancestry. Instead, he took the moral high ground. Angered, he pointed out that "Aryan" was a linguistic term, not a racial one. He then expressed regret that he had no ancestors among the "gifted" Jewish people, although he was pleased to point out that he had many Jewish friends. He was bitterly opposed to the "ignoramus" of a German leader who had usurped and perverted the northern European cultural heritage he so loved.

The Tolkien family endured the war in typical British fashion. The garden was given over to vegetables and chickens to help the family through rationing. Sons Michael and Christopher both served, Michael as an anti-aircraft gunner and Christopher in the Royal Air Force. John turned to the priesthood but had to return to England from his training in

Rome because of the war. Tolkien, meanwhile, served as an air-raid warden and continued with his academic duties. At the same time, he struggled with the sequel to *The Hobbit*, or "the new hobbit" as the Inklings called it. Tolkien felt that writing exposed his innermost self to the world, and it wasn't easy for him. What kept him going was mailing the new chapters to Christopher in service.

By the time the manuscript was finally ready, the now grown-up Rayner Unwin was the one who drove to Oxford in September 1952 to pick up the manuscript. He calculated that the book would cost his company money even if it were successful. His father, who was traveling in Japan at the time, sent back word that he should go ahead and publish it only if he thought it was "a work of genius."

Tolkien had not at all intended his book to be published as a trilogy, and was never thrilled to hear it referred to so, but it ran longer than the famously protracted *War and Peace.* In these years following World War II, paper was expensive because it was in short supply, so it was decided that the work was far too long to publish as one volume. The printing was stretched out over two years so that the volumes appeared in 1954 and 1955. Fans were particularly irate to have to wait out the cliffhanger that ended volume two, now known as *The Two Towers*.

Since he was such a close friend, it's not surprising that C. S. Lewis reviewed the new work with the highest possible praise, but other talented reviewers at the time—such as W. H. Auden in the *Times Book Review*—did the same. Auden, who years earlier had been a student of Tolkien's, was intrigued by *The Lord of the Rings* and began a correspondence with Tolkien. Auden's support meant a great deal to Tolkien, particularly as Tolkien's friendship with Lewis was waning at the time. Praise for the books was not universal, however, and in fact its reviews were highly mixed. Literary critic Edmund Wilson, for example, considered the books absolute trash. Tolkien felt that some of the negative reviews stemmed from the divided printing of the book: critics at the outset were unable to read the book as a unity. On the other hand, he admitted that some of them appeared not to have bothered to read past the first chapter. There is also no question that Lewis's association with the book drew the ire of some reviewers, who lampooned his praise of it. Lewis was himself a highly controversial figure, and reviewers took the occasion to attack him. But then there was simply the complexity and novelty of the book itself. One agenda behind all of Tolkien's efforts was to reclaim fairy tales for an adult readership, but as a result many critics could not decide if the audience for these books was supposed to be children or adults.

As it happened, the publisher did not lose money. Sales were so brisk that Tolkien eventually regretted not having taken early retirement. For the first time in his life, he was comfortably well off. The books' profitability prompted a rapid challenge to the copyright. Houghton Mifflin owned the rights to the hardcover books in the U.S., but another firm, the science-fiction publisher Ace Books, soon brought out a pirated paperback version, which was sold at a greatly reduced price. This lower price was possible because they had no intention of paying royalties to the author. A legal struggle naturally ensued, and the resulting press reports constituted tremendous publicity for the books. A great many people thereby became aware of *The Lord of the Rings* who would not have otherwise. The counter-culture in particular latched onto them, and Tolkien found himself the center of a pop-cult, a mixed blessing since the conservative scholar harbored quite a dislike of hippie culture. Ballantine Books eventually brought out the authorized paperback in 1965 while Ace, pressured by the Science Fiction Writers of America, agreed to pay Tolkien royalties and not to reprint after their existing stock ran out.

The Inside View

At around 5 foot 9 inches, Tolkien was not physically imposing, but he exuded kindness. Neatly dressed and slight of build, he was especially fond of waistcoats. Even as a young professor, he was riveting to his students. He declaimed poetry like a living bard. A fascinating speaker because of the depth of his erudition and his enthusiasm for his subject, he nevertheless spoke so fast and mumbled so frequently that he was difficult to understand. Often, the situation was made worse by the pipe that seldom left his lips.

A doting father, his adult children spoke of him as having been a lifelong friend in addition to a parent. He must have brought a considerable element of magic to his children's lives; in fact, when Michael was filling out the requisite forms for his entry to the military, he put "wizard" as his father's occupation. In later years, Tolkien was a frequent visitor to the home of his son, Father John Tolkien.

Tolkien was a devout Catholic throughout his life, and this perspective gently colored all that he did. His idealization of the Middle Ages stemmed, in part, from his appreciation of a time when a unifying Catholic caste overlaid European society. Similarly, his myth-making, while born from a love of myth, fairy, and language, was for him a religious process. He intended his writings to serve the religious purpose of allusively leading the reader to the ultimate myth—the Gospel. Ever modest, Tolkien believed that a divine muse had given him his works, because he believed that only God could create new things; Tolkien himself was simply the typist. He described his creative process as "sub-creation," a process of ongoing discovery that continually surprised him as much as it did the characters involved. He often didn't know what was going to come next.

A good deal of Tolkien's devotion to the Church came from his profound devotion to his mother. He viewed his mother as a martyr to the faith, believing that her family's rejection and her resulting poverty had been the ultimate cause of her death. He was forever grateful to her for leading him to the Church and did all he could to pass on his faith to his own children. All four of the children attended Catholic boarding school, and he took them frequently for confession and mass despite Edith's disapproval. She did not like confession, but her husband required it for mass to be taken. Tolkien blamed Edith's failure to connect with Catholicism on the poor instruction she had received at the outset of her conversion, but they did eventually reach rapprochement on the subject. She stopped going to mass completely but remained quite involved in other church activities.

Tolkien's general conservatism extended to his religious outlook. Vatican II was a challenge for him. Following the liturgical change from Latin to English that took place following Vatican II, he stubbornly persisted in reciting responses loudly in Latin. This may have been part of the growing rigidity of personality that marked his later years. He claimed otherwise, however; trends, he felt, made the Church less of a refuge against temporal trouble. He clung to loyalty as a virtue during this period of doubt. Loyalty, he wrote to his son Michael, becomes a virtue only when one is tempted to desert it. He showed greater sympathy for the Church's efforts toward ecumenism. An increase in Christian charity could never be remiss.

An early environmentalist, Tolkien found that his love of nature and love of God combined in his antipathy toward industrialization. Machines have their drawbacks, as Tolkien well knew. The Great War was the first war to be mechanized; tanks made their first appearance on the battlefield while planes flew over them. When World War II found his son Christopher in the R.A.F., Tolkien wrote to him that he couldn't be more horrified if a hobbit had learned to ride a Nazgul in order to liberate the Shire. There was more machinery to come: when atomic bombs were dropped on

Japan, Tolkien considered it Babel-building and did not believe that God would look kindly upon it.

Tolkien lamented industrialization's impact on the traditional British life of the countryside, represented in his writings by the hobbits of the Shire. He suffered from the human mistreatment of nature, particularly trees. He rode a bicycle, having given up car ownership as far back as World War II. In part, though, his abandoning the automobile may have been the result of his poor driving, which he satirized in *Mr. Bliss*, the titular character of which crashes into all sorts of things. For his part, Tolkien once crashed into a wall. Edith always worried when her husband was driving.

Despite his skepticism about the advances of the modern world, Tolkien knew the lid couldn't be closed on Pandora's box, just as the door couldn't be closed to knowledge— however badly the technology might be applied in practice.

The Lord of the Rings

Contrary to the claims of some readers, the pre-Christian world of Middle-earth is not pantheistic and in fact appears to be without religion. Tolkien characterized it as a monotheistic world of natural theology. He bristled when hearing that his book was without religion. He also took umbrage at claims that there were no women in *The Lord of the Rings*, which he saw as untrue. He viewed *The Lord of the Rings* as, at heart, a Catholic work. Given his own deep core of faith, it could hardly be anything else. Nevertheless, he did not want his writing to strong-arm the reader, and the divine agency at work within his narrative is hidden, as it is in the biblical Book of Esther.

Tolkien preferred the still, small voice of Elijah to the resounding horns of Sinai. Accordingly, his commitment to myth as his medium was dogged. He repeatedly denied that *The Lord of the Rings* was allegory. The reason is this: allegory intends that *this* particular thing in the story is meant to be *that* particular thing known outside the story. In a way, it is coercive, forcing the reader to see things in a certain way. For example, Lewis's lion in the Narnia books, Aslan, is meant to be understood by the reader as a representation of Christ. Tolkien, in fact, was annoyed with Lewis for engaging in allegory, which he found heavy-handed. (Lewis, for his part, denied that his Narnia books were *only* allegory.) He believed myth to be a more artistically subtle device. Tolkien did not, for instance, intend his War of the Ring to be a battle of good versus evil. He didn't see matters in such black-and-white terms and did not believe in absolute evil. During the Great War, he didn't view the Germans as all bad and the English as all good. In the *Lord of the Rings*, even Sauron, like Lucifer, did not start as evil. Evil for Tolkien was a personal battle within each and every individual. A battle might be won or lost, but the war was unending.

Tolkien's approach to fantasy was not escapist as some critics claimed. To the contrary, his myth was meant to represent the truth of history and the human condition. Thus, it was intended to clarify reality rather than escape from it. It was a sad fact of a fallen world, believed Tolkien, that the exigencies of daily life obscured the human understanding of reality. A good fairy tale, in Tolkien's estimation, restored an appreciation of what was simple and important in human life. As such, it should nourish and restore the soul. Thus, while other characters in *The Lord of the Rings* have no shortage of heroic traits, the central character, Frodo, is the everyman of folk tales. He is unwittingly thrust into events because of seeming happenstance, not due to his heroic qualities. But, like the common British foot soldiers, whom Tolkien marveled were able to carry the day in the trenches, the simple hobbit rises to the occasion.

Whereas the tone of *The Hobbit* is light-hearted and even childish, the Ring saga is darker and more mature, and imbued with echoes from the Great War. Tolkien denied most connections with the war and other externals, not wanting outside referents to color his creation. Nevertheless, reviewers, including his friend Lewis, did not fail to recognize certain associations. Certainly the Shire was Tolkien's beloved West Midlands, and it is hard to see the Dead Marshes and the approach to Mordor as anything but a reflection of the desolate aftermath of the Battle of the Somme. Frodo's "batman" is the ever-faithful Samwise Gamgee, whose company is something of a balm for Frodo's wounded spirit. "Gamgee" was derived from Gamgee Tissue, a surgical dressing invented in 1880 by Dr. Joseph Sampson Gamgee in Tolkien's hometown of Birmingham. The dressing consisted of a thick layer of absorbent cotton wool between two layers of gauze. In Birmingham, it was the common name for cotton wool, the most likely source of Tolkien's usage. There is more, however: Major Leonard Gamgee, a relative of the inventor, was an army surgical officer at the Birmingham hospital where Tolkien convalesced upon first arriving back in England. Rob Gilson's sister rolled bandages for Major Gamgee, but it's not certain whether Tolkien specifically knew of him. He did mention that, in his childhood, there was a Dr.

Gamgee in Birmingham whom he believed was a relative of the inventor of Gamgee tissue.

Body of Work

It is important not to overlook Tolkien's scholarly contributions, particularly his 1936 lecture to the British Academy in London, "Beowulf: The Monsters and the Critics," which was quite influential in the field of Beowulf studies. In it, he argued against prior scholarship that was primarily interested in mining the poem for information about its sources. Instead, he defended its artistic unity and integrity. Tolkien's scholarly essays were reprinted in *The Monsters and the Critics and Other Essays.* In addition, he and his son Christopher published translations of such Middle English works as the *Andree Wisse, Sir Gawain and the Green Knight, Sir Orfeo*, and *The Pearl.* While in many ways a masterful teacher, Tolkien never fulfilled his potential as an academic researcher. Because of his perfectionism, he kept reworking his academic writings so that many of them never reached publication at all.

The situation is considerably better with his popular writings. Most, but not all, of his popular work is a part of his "legendarium," the web of mythology that comprised his recounting of a fictional period in Earth's history. *The Hobbit* and *The Lord of the Rings* are centerpieces of that legendarium, but *The Hobbit* was not originally so. Because of what happened in *The Lord of the Rings, The Hobbit* came to be pulled into the legendarium. It was *The Silmarillion*, finally published in 1977 and edited by Christopher Tolkien, that was really intended to form its core. In 1980, Christopher published his father's *Unfinished Tales of Númenor and Middle-earth*. Another work belonging to the legendarium but published separately was *The Adventures of Tom Bombadil* (1962), a collection of poetry, including some about the eponymous character first met in *The Lord of the Rings*.

In addition to the legendarium, there are a few stories that are versions of the stories Tolkien told his children, such as *Mr. Bliss* and *Roverandom*. *The Father Christmas Letters* were published in 1976. Tolkien's other stories that were not a part of the legendarium include the well-known *Farmer Giles of Ham*, *Leaf by Niggle*, and *Smith of Wootton Major*, but also the lesser-known *Imram*, *The Homecoming of Beorhtnoth Beorhthelm's Son*, and *The Lay of Aotrou and Itroun*.

Finally, Christopher edited and published a 12-volume *History of Middle-earth*, a massive undertaking that began in 1983 and concluded in 1997.

The Fading Light

Tolkien retired from Oxford in 1959 at the age of sixty-seven, shortly before sales of his books exploded. He then achieved cult-like status. He was both wary and appreciative of his newfound notoriety. Increasingly, phone calls from America at all hours of the night became overly intrusive, and he unlisted his number, finally changing his address altogether. In any event, Oxford was becoming too inconvenient for a non-driver. Tolkien and Edith moved to a one-story bungalow in Bournemouth, a seaside town popular with retirees, in 1968. It was Edith's choice of location. Edith had always had delicate health and was now suffering from mobility issues due to arthritis. She had never liked the academic stuffiness of Oxford, so Tolkien considered the move to Bournemouth compensation for her years of putting up with Oxford.

Edith died after a brief illness in November 1971 at the age of eighty-two. Tolkien had the name "Lúthien" inscribed on her tombstone, hearkening back to the beautiful girl who had danced for him in the woods long before. His marriage to Edith had known trials and dark times. When she married, Edith had given up her planned career as a pianist. Instead, her life had revolved around home and family, and her shyness in the rarified air of Oxford had kept her even more tied to the house. Edith hadn't had an easy time as a Catholic, and she had often found excuses to avoid going to mass. Her initial instruction in the faith had been poor, and Tolkien had not been able to do more than communicate to her his love for the religion, which she had neither understood nor shared. In many ways, he had shut her out from his intellectual life and circles of male camaraderie, which was not so unusual in those days. Even their schedules had differed, with Tolkien staying up until the early morning hours to work on his various pursuits. There was, in fact, much that she had resented. Even so, no one had ever doubted the affection the two shared. They had forged a bond in their youth that was challenged over time but remained unbroken. Lúthien she would always be to him. Having lost her, he felt maimed and adrift.

Tolkien now moved back to Oxford, where he was offered rooms on campus. There he unsuccessfully attempted to complete more of his mythic writings. He arranged for Christopher to assume the task if he died prior to finishing it. Without Edith and his former circles of friends, Tolkien was often lonely, though rarely alone. In 1972 he was pleased to receive an honorary doctorate from Oxford in acknowledgement of his work in philology; he had been rather taken aback when he had received an honorary Doctor of Letters in Belgium and been introduced as the creator of

Bilbo Baggins. For Tolkien, all of his writing was rooted in philology, and he preferred that it be understood that way.

In 1973 Tolkien was named a Commander of the British Empire (CBE) by Queen Elizabeth II in a ceremony at Buckingham Palace. But then, in August 1973, he suddenly took ill when visiting in Bournemouth. He died at the age of eighty-one on September 2, 1973, of a bleeding gastric ulcer and pneumonia. He and Edith currently rest together in a single grave in the Catholic section of a cemetery in the northern suburbs of Oxford—and on the stone, together with "Lúthien," is now written "Beren."

Please enjoy the first two chapters of Pope Francis: Pastor of Mercy, written by Michael J. Ruszala, as available from Wyatt North Publishing.

Pope Francis: Pastor of Mercy

Chapter 1

There is something about Pope Francis that captivates and delights people, even people who hardly know anything about him. He was elected in only two days of the conclave, yet many who tried their hand at speculating on who the next pope might be barely included him on their lists. The evening of Wednesday, March 13, 2013, the traditional white smoke poured out from the chimney of the Sistine Chapel and spread throughout the world by way of television, Internet, radio, and social media, signaling the beginning of a new papacy.

As the light of day waned from the Eternal City, some 150,000 people gathered watching intently for any movement behind the curtained door to the loggia of St. Peter's. A little after 8:00 p.m., the doors swung open and Cardinal Tauran emerged to pronounce the traditional and joyous Latin formula to introduce the new Bishop of Rome: "Annuncio vobis gaudium magnum; habemus papam!" ("I announce to you a great joy: we have a pope!") He then announced the new Holy Father's identity: "Cardinalem Bergoglio..."

The name Bergoglio, stirred up confusion among most of the faithful who flooded the square that were even more clueless than the television announcers were, who scrambled to figure out who exactly the new pope was. Pausing briefly, Cardinal

Tauran continued by announcing the name of the new pope: "...qui sibi nomen imposuit Franciscum" ("who takes for himself the name Francis"). Whoever this man may be, his name choice resonated with all, and the crowd erupted with jubilant cheers. A few moments passed before the television announcers and their support teams informed their global audiences that the man who was about to walk onto the loggia dressed in white was Cardinal Jorge Mario Bergoglio, age 76, of Buenos Aires, Argentina.

To add to the bewilderment and kindling curiosity, when the new pope stepped out to the thunderous applause of the crowd in St. Peter's Square, he did not give the expected papal gesture of outstretched arms. Instead, he gave only a simple and modest wave. Also, before giving his first apostolic blessing, he bowed asking the faithful, from the least to the greatest, to silently pray for him. These acts were only the beginning of many more words and gestures, such as taking a seat on the bus with the cardinals, refusing a popemobile with bulletproof glass, and paying his own hotel bill after his election, that would raise eyebrows among some familiar with papal customs and delight the masses.

Is he making a pointed critique of previous pontificates? Is he simply posturing a persona to the world at large to make a point? The study of the life of Jorge Mario Bergoglio gives a clear answer, and the answer is no. This is simply who he is as a man and as a priest. The example of his thought- provoking gestures flows from his character, his life experiences, his religious vocation, and his spirituality. This book uncovers the life of the 266th Bishop of Rome, Jorge Mario Bergoglio, also known as Father Jorge, a name he preferred even while he was an archbishop and cardinal.

What exactly do people find so attractive about Pope Francis? Aldo Cagnoli, a layman who developed a friendship with the Pope when he was serving as a cardinal, shares the following: "The greatness of the man, in my humble opinion lies not in building walls or seeking refuge behind his wisdom and office, but rather in dealing with everyone judiciously, respectfully, and with humility, being willing to learn at any moment of life; that is what Father Bergoglio means to me" (as quoted in Ch. 12 of Pope Francis: Conversations with Jorge Bergoglio, previously published as El Jesuita [The Jesuit]).

At World Youth Day 2013, in Rio de Janeiro, Brazil, three million young people came out to celebrate their faith with

Pope Francis. Doug Barry, from EWTN's Life on the Rock, interviewed youth at the event on what features stood out to them about Pope Francis. The young people seemed most touched by his authenticity. One young woman from St. Louis said, "He really knows his audience. He doesn't just say things to say things... And he is really sincere and genuine in all that he does." A friend agreed: "He was looking out into the crowd and it felt like he was looking at each one of us...." A young man from Canada weighed in: "You can actually relate to [him]... for example, last night he was talking about the World Cup and athletes." A young woman added, "I feel he means what he says... he practices what he preaches... he states that he's there for the poor and he actually means it."

The Holy Spirit guided the College of Cardinals in its election of Pope Francis to meet the needs of the Church following the historic resignation of Pope Benedict XVI due to old age. Representing the growth and demographic shift in the Church throughout the world and especially in the Southern Hemisphere, Pope Francis is the first non-European pope in almost 1,300 years. He is also the first Jesuit pope. Pope Francis comes with a different background and set of experiences. Both as archbishop and as pope, his flock knows him for his humility, ascetic frugality in solidarity with the poor, and closeness. He was born in Buenos Aires to a family of Italian immigrants, earned a diploma in chemistry, and followed a priestly vocation in the Jesuit order after an experience of God's mercy while receiving the sacrament of Reconciliation. Even though he is known for his smile and humor, the world also recognizes Pope Francis as a stern figure that stands against the evils of the world and challenges powerful government officials, when necessary.

The Church he leads is one that has been burdened in the West by the aftermath of sex abuse scandals and increased secularism. It is also a Church that is experiencing shifting in numbers out of the West and is being challenged with religious persecution in the Middle East, Asia, and Africa. The Vatican that Pope Francis has inherited is plagued by cronyism and scandal. This Holy Father knows, however, that his job is not merely about numbers, politics, or even success. He steers clear of pessimism knowing that he is the head of Christ's Body on earth and works with Christ's grace. This is the man God has chosen in these times to lead his flock.

Chapter 2: Early Life in Argentina

Jorge Mario Bergoglio was born on December 17, 1936, in the Flores district of Buenos Aires. The district was a countryside locale outside the main city during the nineteenth century and many rich people in its early days called this place home. By the time Jorge was born, Flores was incorporated into the city of Buenos Aires and became a middle class neighborhood. Flores is also the home of the beautiful Romantic-styled Basilica of San José de Flores, built in 1831, with its dome over the altar, spire over the entrance, and columns at its facade. It was the Bergoglios' parish church and had much significance in Jorge's life.

Jorge's father's family had arrived in Argentina in 1929, immigrating from Piedimonte in northern Italy. They were not the only ones immigrating to the country. In the late nineteenth century, Argentina became industrialized and the government promoted immigration from Europe. During that time, the land prospered and Buenos Aires earned the moniker "Paris of the South." In the late nineteenth and early twentieth centuries waves of immigrants from Italy, Spain, and other European countries came off ships in the port of Buenos Aires. Three of Jorge's great uncles were the first in the family to immigrate to Argentina in 1922 searching for better employment opportunities after World War I. They established a paving company in Buenos Aires and built a four-story building for their company with the city's first elevator. Jorge's father and paternal grandparents followed the brothers in order to keep the family together and to escape Mussolini's fascist regime in Italy. Jorge's father and grandfather also helped with the business for a time. His father, Mario, who had been an accountant for a rail company in Italy, provided similar services for the family business (Cardinal Bergoglio recalls more on the story of his family's immigration and his early life in Ch. 1 of Conversations with Jorge Bergoglio).

Providentially, the Bergoglios were long delayed in liquidating their assets in Italy; this forced them to miss the ship they planned to sail on, the doomed Pricipessa Mafalda, which sank off the northern coast of Brazil before reaching Buenos Aires. The family took the Giulio Cesare instead and arrived safely in Argentina with Jorge's Grandma Rosa. Grandma Rosa wore a fur coat stuffed with the money the family brought with them from Italy. Economic hard times eventually hit Argentina in 1932 and the family's paving business went under, but the Bergoglio brothers began anew.

Jorge's father, Mario, met his mother Regina at Mass in 1934. Regina was born in Argentina, but her parents were also Italian immigrants. Mario and Regina married the following year after meeting. Jorge, the eldest of their five children, was born in 1936. Jorge fondly recalls his mother gathering the children around the radio on Sunday afternoons to listen to opera and explain the story. A true porteño, as the inhabitants of the port city of Buenos Aires are called, Jorge liked to play soccer, listen to Latin music, and dance the tango. Jorge's paternal grandparents lived around the corner from his home. He greatly admired his Grandma Rosa, and keeps her written prayer for her grandchildren with him until this day. Jorge recalls that while his grandparents kept their personal conversations in Piedmontese, Mario chose mostly to speak Spanish, preferring to look forward rather than back. Still, Jorge grew up speaking both Italian and Spanish.

Upon entering secondary school at the age of thirteen, his father insisted that Jorge begin work even though the family, in their modest lifestyle, was not particularly in need of extra income. Mario Bergoglio wanted to teach the boy the value of work and found several jobs for him during his adolescent years. Jorge worked in a hosiery factory for several years as a cleaner and at a desk. When he entered technical school to study food chemistry, Jorge found a job working in a laboratory. He worked under a woman who always challenged him to do his work thoroughly. He remembers her, though, with both fondness and sorrow. Years later, she was kidnapped and murdered along with members of her family because of her political views during the Dirty War, a conflict in the 1970's and 80's between the military dictatorship and guerrilla fighters in which thousands of Argentineans disappeared.

Initially unhappy with his father's decision to make him work, Jorge recalls later in his life that work was a valuable formative experience for him that taught him responsibility, realism, and how the world operated. He learned that a person's self worth often comes from their work, which led him to become committed later in life to promote a just culture of work rather than simply encouraging charity or entitlement. He believes that people need meaningful work in order to thrive. During his boyhood through his priestly ministry, he experienced the gulf in Argentina between the poor and the well off, which left the poor having few opportunities for gainful employment.

At the age of twenty-one, Jorge became dangerously ill. He was diagnosed with severe pneumonia and cysts. Part of his upper right lung was removed, and each day Jorge endured the pain and discomfort of saline fluid pumped through his chest to clear his system. Jorge remembers that the only person that was able to comfort him during this time was a religious sister who had catechized him from childhood, Sister Dolores. She exposed him to the true meaning of suffering with this simple statement: "You are imitating Christ." This stuck with him, and his sufferings during that time served as a crucible for his character, teaching him how to distinguish what is important in life from what is not. He was being prepared for what God was calling him to do in life, his vocation.

Made in the USA
Coppell, TX
03 December 2019

12334297R00066